A Simple Seagrass

by Camille Klump

Illustrated by
Mike Roberts &
Dawn Witherington

Acknowledgements

Thank you to my incredible team of artists Mike Roberts, and Dawn Witherington, for helping to bring my green vision to life. I am grateful to my daughter Chebioam Vieira whose creative vision produced a stunning design for the author's website and the book cover. I wrote A Simple Seagrass to help children understand how important seagrasses are in helping to maintain clean and healthy oceans, and I wanted to highlight how its loss will affect the many creatures that depend on it for survival. I was so humbled to receive the endorsement of Mr. Peter A. Clark, the president and founder of Tampa Bay Watch. A special thank you to his staff for providing technical support and images of successful seagrass restoration projects around Tampa Bay. Finally, without the input of the editors and interior layout designer, the final touches on this book would not have been possible.

FOREWORD

We all enjoy living close to the coast and appreciate a day at the beach. Because of our coastal location the Tampa Bay area is considered one of the most vulnerable communities to sea level rise. Because of that, Tampa Bay Watch's habitat restoration efforts have changed to accommodate the expected future sea-level rise and increased storm activity. A small amount of natural coastal habitat can provide important storm protection for our communities.

Coastal habitat restoration projects, such as salt marsh and oysters, are a tool for restoring our lost habitat and ensure long term protection of our shorelines. Tampa Bay Watch utilizes native plants in a variety of restoration projects through community planting events and our Bay Grasses in Classes program. These hands-on programs provide students the opportunity to restore coastal habitats with local bay area scientists. Our Bay Grasses in Classes allows middle and high school students the

chance to maintain and grow native wetland grasses at
their school to be replanted into targeted coastal areas
- which has resulted in the restoration of more than 171
acres around Tampa Bay.

There is a world of discovery and exploration outdoors:
including a wide variety of wildlife, hiking, boating,
snorkeling, and kayak adventures to name just a few.
It's an amazing experience to see marine life up close,
witness the fragility of our ecosystem and learn the
effects of conservation and restoration projects. A goal
of Tampa Bay Watch is for young and old to respect the
environment and understand the importance of keeping
the Tampa Bay estuary clean and healthy for generations
to come. The experiences and knowledge gained for all
ages will provide a lifetime of environmental stewardship.

Peter A. Clark,
President and Founder
Tampa Bay Watch

Did you know many countries around the world are trying to protect seagrasses?

What is seagrass, and why is seagrass important? What role does it play, and why is it disappearing?

WHAT IS SEAGRASS?

Seagrasses are flowering plants that also produce seeds. They grow on the seabed and survive submerged in water. Scientists say that seagrasses are about seventy million to one hundred million years old. The survival of many sea creatures depends on healthy seagrass colonies. They use seagrass leaves for food and as their home.

WHY IS SEAGRASS IMPORTANT?

Marine animals, like sea squirts and mollusks, lay their eggs on seagrass leaves. In Florida, manatees, parrotfish, and green turtles feed on seagrass.

Anemones and sponges, for example, use seagrasses as their habitats, or places to live. They attach themselves to the leaves of seagrasses. Sea urchins, seahorses, pipefish, lizard fish, bottlenose dolphins, grunts, snapper, and stingrays can all be found in seagrass meadows.

However, rapid loss of seagrasses in places like Florida is threatening the manatee population. It is also becoming more difficult for other sea creatures to survive. They are losing their habitats and major food source.

Fish like grunts and snook have young that grow up in seagrass beds. They feed on smaller animals that also live between the seagrass blades. Sport fishermen and restaurants depend on these and other fish found among seagrasses. The loss of seagrasses will mean less fish.

Birds also use seagrass beds for foraging and feeding. These include egrets, herons, and brown pelicans.

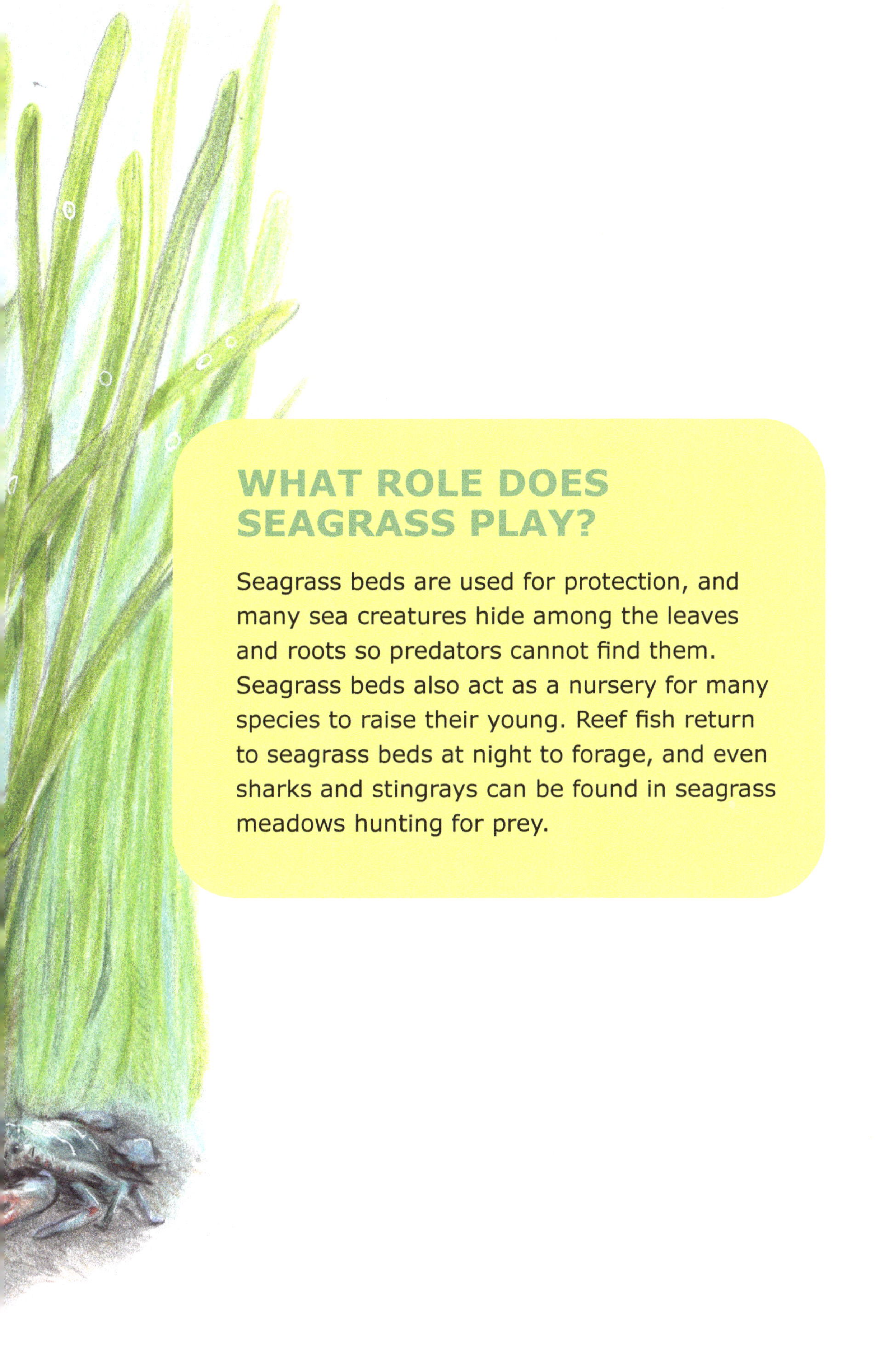

WHAT ROLE DOES SEAGRASS PLAY?

Seagrass beds are used for protection, and many sea creatures hide among the leaves and roots so predators cannot find them. Seagrass beds also act as a nursery for many species to raise their young. Reef fish return to seagrass beds at night to forage, and even sharks and stingrays can be found in seagrass meadows hunting for prey.

Like all other plants, seagrasses turn nutrients and sunlight into organic matter. They use sunlight to turn carbon dioxide and water into sugar and oxygen. This process of photosynthesis benefits other marine life and plants.

Seagrasses also trap sediment suspended in the water column to help water stay clear. Clear water has another important function: it allows more sunlight to pass through. Additional light encourages photosynthesis—the process that produces oxygen in the water.

Other animals and plants rely on the oxygen produced by seagrasses. Even the roots and stems of seagrasses store nutrients.

Seagrasses serve many other essential functions. They absorb carbon dioxide in the water, which helps to slow the effects of climate change. Seagrasses also act as a buffer against wave energy that would otherwise hurt the habitats of many marine animals. Seagrasses help to stabilize the seafloor, similar to how land grasses help fight erosion. They protect coastal areas from the effects of waves and strong currents. Seagrasses also help to filter storm water runoff.

The benefits of seagrasses continue even after they die. When organisms decompose, they produce organic matter known as detritus.
It falls to the seafloor, providing food for other creatures like sea worms, sea cucumbers, and crabs. Decomposed seagrass releases nutrients like nitrogen and phosphorus, which marine plants and creatures reabsorb. These chemicals aid their growth cycle.

WHAT IS CAUSING THE LOSS OF SEAGRASS?

Boat propellers from recreational craft are ripping up sea grass from the ocean floor. Over time, the seabed can become scarred. A damaged seabed makes it impossible for grass to regrow and spread. Entire seagrass meadows have been lost because of this.

Human activity, such as building too close to the coastline, can cause the loss of seagrass. Pollution due to pesticides is also to blame. Excess nitrogen from fertilizers and contaminated wastewater also has a negative effect on the health of seagrass.

WHAT CAN I DO TO HELP STOP THIS ENVIRONMENTAL CRISIS?

You can volunteer to help replant endangered seagrasses around shores and coastlines in your own communities. These are called restoration projects.

Bay Grasses in Classes

You can also participate in a Bay Grasses in Classes (BGIC) program, which occur in outdoor seagrass nurseries. Find out if your school or community supports this type of volunteer program. This environmental project will teach you how to take care of seagrasses until they are ready to be replanted in areas designated for restoration.

When the grass is ready for replanting, you can join adults, scientists and other volunteers at a restoration site. These are areas that have lost seagrass meadows. Some successful program sites include Mac Dill Air Force Base, Safety Harbor, and Cockroach Bay.

Cockroach Bay
Mac Dill shoreline

A SUMMARY OF SEAGRASSES

Like all plants, seagrasses turn nutrients and sunlight into organic matter. Manatees, green turtles, and other undersea grazers use these plants for food. Certain fish like grunts and snook, found in Florida's waters, have young that grow up in seagrass beds. They feed on smaller animals that also live between the seagrass blades. These grasses trap sediment, helping the water stay clear, which allows more sunlight to pass through. More light helps photosynthesis, the process that produces oxygen in the water, which in turn benefits other marine animals. Seagrasses also act as a buffer against wave energy that would otherwise erode the habitats of many marine animals.

Florida Manatee

Great Egret

Southern Stingray

Stoplight Parrotfish

French Grunt

Green Turtle

Common Snook

Pink Shrimp

Purple Sea Urchin

Juvenile Spiny Lobster

Thinstripe Hermit Crab

Blue Crab

TYPES OF SEAGRASSES FOUND IN FLORIDA

Manatee grass has long tube-shaped leaves and is found in many of Florida's estuaries. These grasses are a manatee's favorite food. Did you know that pollution and human activity are destroying these grasses, making it more difficult for Florida's manatees to find food?

Turtle grass is the largest of the seagrasses found in Florida. Turtle grass has large, long leaves and thick roots that grow deep in the ground. Many sea creatures use its leaves and roots for food and shelter. Turtle grass meadows are found in places like the Florida Keys and Florida Bay. Did you know these grasses produce white or pink flowers in spring and summer, and green sea turtles can be found grazing in the grass beds?

Shoal grass is said to most resemble land grass with flat, narrow, blade-like leaves, with three points at the tip of each blade. It grows in estuarine waters but will survive in much saltier areas. Shoal grass grows well and quickly in areas that have been disturbed and tolerates a wide range of temperatures. Parrotfish and sea urchins feed on these grasses. Did you know shoal grass produces an egg-shaped fruit that grows to only about two millimeters in size?

Star grass is smaller than the other grasses and has short oval leaves that grow in a star-shaped cluster of four to eight leaves. It can be found growing below other seagrasses. Did you know it prefers sandy or muddy bottoms and grows in water as deep as one hundred and thirty feet.

Johnson's seagrass grows in the Indian River lagoon. It is a small grass with oval-shaped leaves, smooth edges, and a pointed tip. Did you know green sea turtles and manatees feed on these leaves?

Widgeon grass can be found in Florida's estuaries. Its leaf blades are wide at the base and narrow down to a long-pointed tip. Did you know the pollen from widgeon grass is released at the surface of the water?

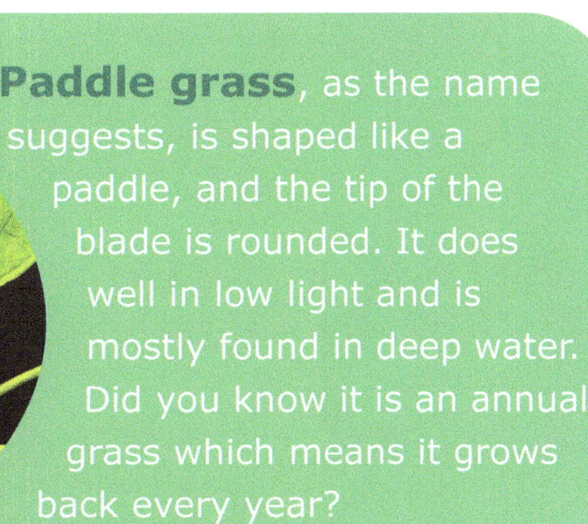

Paddle grass, as the name suggests, is shaped like a paddle, and the tip of the blade is rounded. It does well in low light and is mostly found in deep water. Did you know it is an annual grass which means it grows back every year?

HOW SEAGRASSES FORM PART OF FLORIDA'S ECOSYSTEMS

SUBTIDAL LAGOON

A lagoon is a shallow body of water, separated from larger bodies of water by a natural barrier. Florida has several long lagoons that line the state's coast. You can find certain species of seagrasses in Florida's lagoons. Try to identify the aquatic lagoon life you see in the picture.

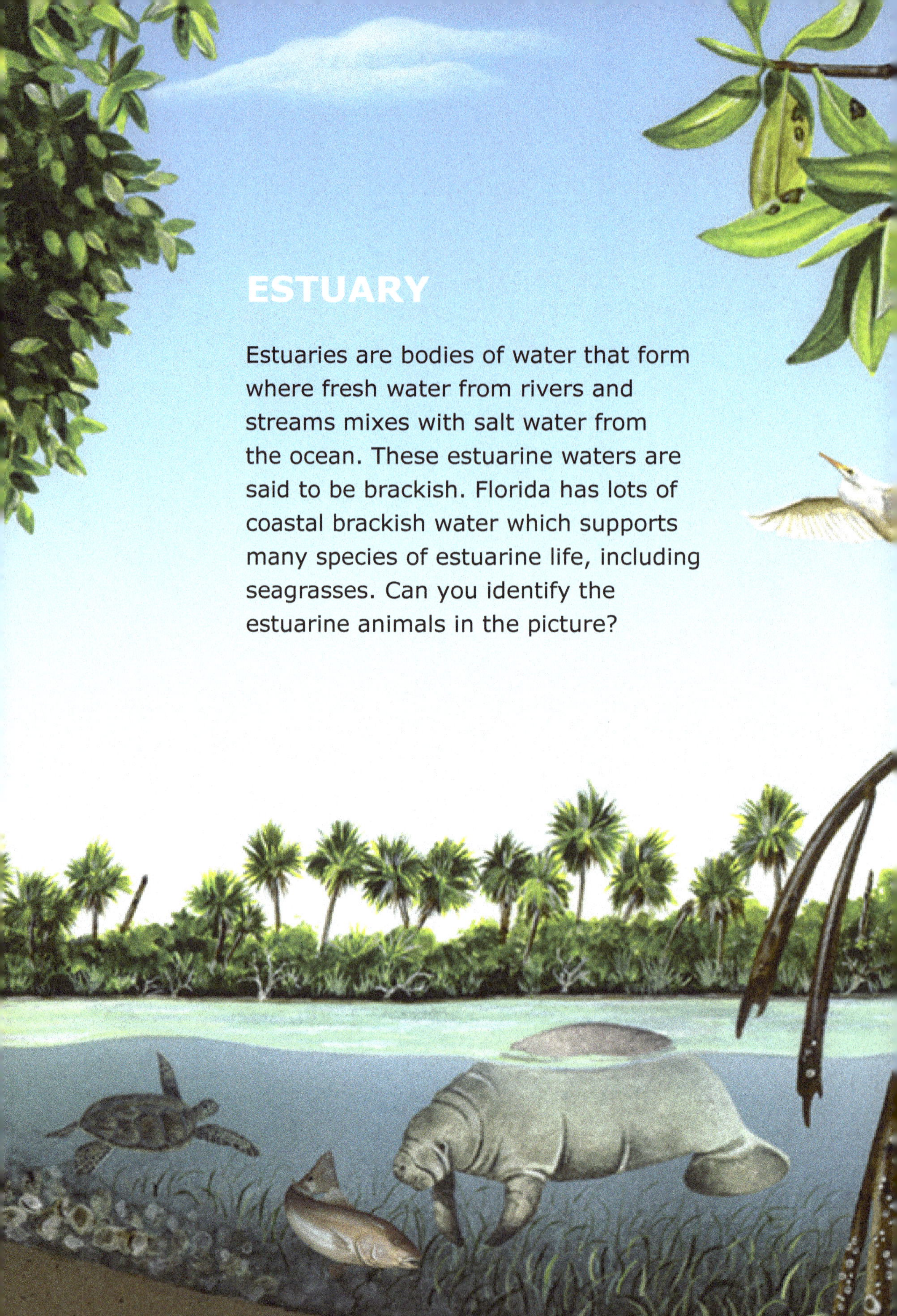

ESTUARY

Estuaries are bodies of water that form where fresh water from rivers and streams mixes with salt water from the ocean. These estuarine waters are said to be brackish. Florida has lots of coastal brackish water which supports many species of estuarine life, including seagrasses. Can you identify the estuarine animals in the picture?

BACK REEF

The shallow area between the highest
point of a reef and a lagoon is known as
a back reef. It extends from the coast to
the coral reef "crest"—the highest point.
A back reef is protected from waves.
Coastal marine habitats are found here,
such as mangroves and seagrasses.

HERE IS A POEM TO HELP YOU REMEMBER
WHAT YOU JUST LEARNT.

A SIMPLE SEAGRASS

In the ocean, along coastlines, in bays and muddy ground
The world's precious seagrasses were once abundantly found.

But now sea grass is dying, and we are left just with sand
So, we're forced to feed our manatees lettuce by hand.
The sea cows don't seem to enjoy this new snack.
Much happier they'd be if their grass beds came back.

Do you know there now exists an environmental plan
To replant endangered seagrasses wherever we can?

You may ask why it matters, and what good is sea grass?
Well, it's a home for such creatures as turtles and bass.
Our precious seagrass cleans and filters the air.
And their roots protect sea creatures—are you aware?

To you they may seem
like no more than a weed,
But it's on rich seagrass
that sea urchins do feed.
Those leaves then decay
and fall to the ocean floor,
They will become a meal
for crabs, worms, and
many more!

In grass beds manatees eat breed, and play.
To frolic in December and stay until May,
They gobble up hundreds of pounds every day—
These grass beds are a haven for sharks and stingrays!

But pesticides slowly have seeped in our Bay.
And pollution destroys more of the grass every day.
The paddle, star, Johnson, and widgeon grass
Are ripped from the seabed as speeding boats pass
Once a buffer, this grass is now torn from the ground.
Onto our shores heavy winds now pound and pound.

Gone are shoal turtle and manatee grass,
And with it the habitat of snappers and bass.

Our oceans need seagrass to stay healthy and clear.
Cloudy water blocks sunlight each day of the year
Plants and sea creatures depend on this light
The loss of our seagrass what a terrible plight!

To harvest and replant are lessons taught in class,
For children to help restore our precious seagrass.
To take the grass plugs to areas that's bare
The moral of this story I hope you will share.

If we want to live greener, then let's do a little bit more
To protect our seagrasses on ocean, coast, and shore.

CONCLUSION

You were presented with a quick study about seagrasses in Florida, but seagrasses can be found in oceans and bays all around the world. Climate change is happening, but don't let it scare you. One example of climate change is the warming of the world's oceans. Each of us can do something to help protect the environment, no matter how small. Look for conservation projects in your own community. Grow wildflowers to help attract more pollinators like bees and butterflies. Recycle. Learn how oyster gardens that use recycled oyster shells help to purify polluted ocean water. Plant a tree to increase oxygen. You can even plant seagrasses to help protect all the many creatures described in this book.

Certificate

of

Achievement

This certificate is presented to:

....

**For completing a first study
on Seagrasses.**

Date..

ABOUT ME
(AND MY BOOKS)

My love of nature and the changing climate inspired me to write several children's books about the urgency of protecting our natural resources.
I hope my stories might one day inspire "green children" everywhere.

My books are available on Amazon and major bookstores or through my website:
www.camilleklump.com

The Oyster Garden is endorsed by the city of Oldsmar in Florida. It is a poetry-styled narrative for ages 6 to 9. Beautiful illustrations demonstrate how vertical oyster gardens using recycled oyster shells are made to help filter polluted ocean water. Realistic drawings will help children discover the variety of creatures that benefit from cleaner oceans.

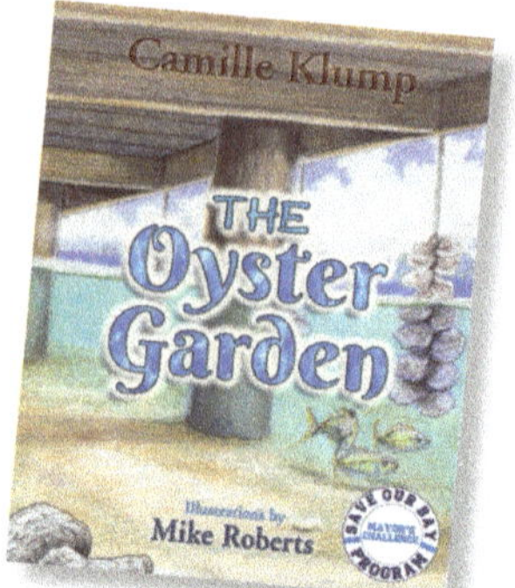

A Code Red Christmas s a wonderfully illustrated fairy tale for ages 8 to 12 that reveals how the destruction of the Amazon rainforest is causing the warming of the North Pole.
This delightful story is filled with humor, suspense, and adventure as Santa's helpers try to save the rainforest in time for Christmas.

Four Paws and a Tale addresses the challenges of growing up. It is based on the true story of a young military family who learns to overcome the difficulties of deployments and overseas assignments. Within its pages, are lessons on separation, love, forgiveness, loyalty, service, letting go, and the unbreakable bond between a dog and its owner.
This book is suitable for ages 9 to 13.

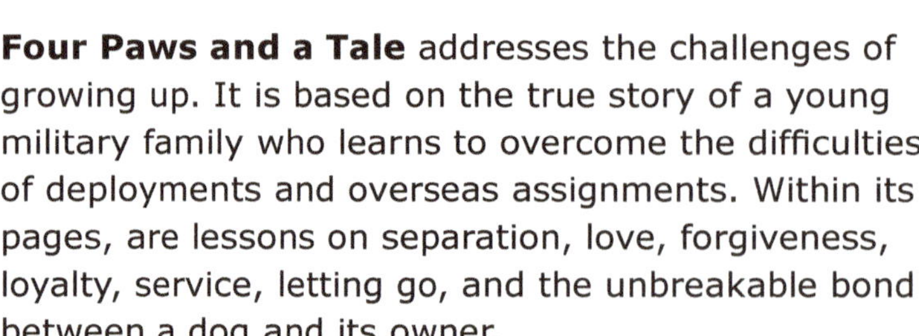

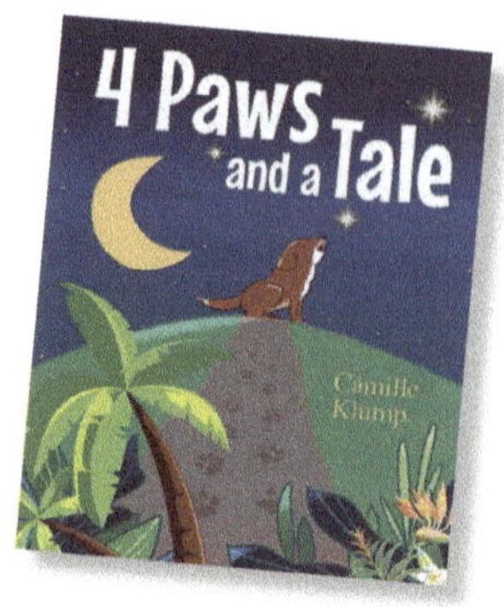